Great Expectations

A Personal Keepsake Journal

For

_____

_____

_____

Date

_____

Great Expectations

A Pregnancy Journal

*A special place to record
the precious times,
prayers, thoughts, feelings
and events that will
be forever cherished!*

*Compiled & Edited by
Caroline Brownlow*

The moment a child is born, the mother is also born. She never existed before. The woman existed, but the mother, never. A mother is something absolutely new.

Rajneesh

You are bone of my bones,
and flesh of my flesh.

Genesis 2:23

_____
_____
_____
_____
_____
_____
_____
_____
_____
_____
_____
_____
_____
_____
_____
_____
_____
_____
_____
_____
_____
_____
_____
_____
_____
_____
_____
_____
_____

A Letter to My Child...

_____

_____

_____

_____

_____

_____

_____

_____

_____

_____

_____

_____

_____

_____

_____

_____

_____

_____

_____

_____

_____

_____

_____

_____

_____

_____

_____

The first handshake in life is the greatest of all:
the clasp of an infant's hand around the finger of a parent.

Anonymous

A babe is nothing but a bundle
of possibilities.

Henry Ward Beecher

A PRAYER FOR MY CHILD

Dear God...

_____

_____

_____

_____

_____

_____

_____

_____

_____

_____

_____

_____

_____

_____

_____

_____

_____

_____

_____

_____

_____

_____

_____

_____

_____

Every baby needs a lap.

Henry Robin

_____
_____
_____
_____
_____
_____
_____
_____
_____
_____
_____
_____
_____
_____
_____
_____
_____
_____
_____
_____
_____
_____
_____
_____

We have been given a great treasure in the form of our children; let us attend to them with great care.

John Chrysostom

Babies are such a nice way to start people.

Don Herold

If men bore the children,
there would be only one born per family.
Anonymous

_____

_____

_____

_____

_____

_____

_____

_____

_____

_____

_____

_____

_____

_____

_____

_____

_____

_____

_____

_____

_____

_____

_____

_____

A Letter to My Child...

_____

_____

_____

_____

_____

_____

_____

_____

_____

_____

_____

_____

_____

_____

_____

_____

_____

_____

_____

_____

_____

_____

_____

_____

_____

I love little children, and it is not a slight thing when they, who are fresh from God, love us.

Charles Dickens

_____

_____

_____

_____

_____

_____

_____

_____

_____

_____

_____

_____

_____

_____

_____

_____

_____

_____

_____

_____

_____

_____

_____

_____

_____

_____

_____

A baby will make love stronger, days shorter, nights longer, bankroll smaller, home happier, clothes shabbier, the past forgotten, and the future worth living for.

Anonymous

_____

_____

_____

_____

_____

_____

_____

_____

_____

_____

_____

_____

_____

_____

_____

_____

_____

_____

_____

_____

_____

_____

_____

_____

Children are always the only future the
human race has; teach them well.

Anonymous

Babies are like sponges. They absorb all your strength and leave you limp. But give them a squeeze and you get it all back.

Anonymous

I prayed for this child, and the Lord has
granted me what I asked of him.

1Samuel 1:27

*More babies are spoiled because the mother
won't spank Grandma.*

Anonymous

_____
_____
_____
_____
_____
_____
_____
_____
_____
_____
_____
_____
_____
_____
_____
_____
_____
_____
_____
_____
_____
_____
_____
_____
_____

To My Child

You are the trip I did not take;
You are the pearls I cannot buy;
You are my blue Italian lake;
You are my piece of foreign sky.

Anne Campbell

_____

_____

_____

_____

_____

_____

_____

_____

_____

_____

_____

_____

_____

_____

_____

_____

_____

_____

_____

_____

_____

_____

Here we have a baby.
It is composed of a bald head
and a pair of lungs.

Eugene Field

A baby is God's opinion that
the world should go on.
Carl Sandburg

A Letter to My Child...

_____

_____

_____

_____

_____

_____

_____

_____

_____

_____

_____

_____

_____

_____

_____

_____

_____

_____

_____

_____

_____

_____

_____

_____

*Children need love, especially
when they do not deserve it.*

Harold S. Hulbert

_____

_____

_____

_____

_____

_____

_____

_____

_____

_____

_____

_____

_____

_____

_____

_____

_____

_____

_____

_____

_____

_____

_____

_____

_____

_____

A babe in a house is a well-spring of pleasure,
a messenger of peace and love,
a resting place for innocence on earth,
a link between angels and men.

Martin F. Tupper

_____

_____

_____

_____

_____

_____

_____

_____

_____

_____

_____

_____

_____

_____

_____

_____

_____

_____

_____

_____

_____

_____

_____

_____

_____

_____

For you created my inmost being;
you knit me together in my mother's womb.

Psalm 139:13

_____
_____
_____
_____
_____
_____
_____
_____
_____
_____
_____
_____
_____
_____
_____
_____
_____
_____
_____
_____
_____
_____
_____
_____
_____
_____
_____

A sweet child is the
sweetest thing in nature.

Charles Lamb

*Give a little love to a child,
and you get a great deal back.*

John Ruskin

Sleep.

During his first year this should be the baby's chief occupation.

Mary L. Read

Making the decision to have a child is momentous-
it is to decide forever to have your heart
go walking around outside your body.

Elizabeth Stone

There are 152 distinctly different ways of
holding a baby – and all are right.

Heywood Broun

We will proclaim Your righteousness to a people yet unborn.
Future generations will hear about the Lord.

Psalm 22:30, 31

_____

_____

_____

_____

_____

_____

_____

_____

_____

_____

_____

_____

_____

_____

_____

_____

_____

_____

_____

_____

_____

_____

_____

_____

_____

_____

A PRAYER FOR MY CHILD

Dear God...

_____
_____
_____
_____
_____
_____
_____
_____
_____
_____
_____
_____
_____
_____
_____
_____
_____
_____
_____
_____
_____
_____
_____
_____
_____
_____
_____
_____

No one who has ever brought up a child can doubt for a
moment that love is literally the life-giving
fluid of human existence.

Dr. Smiley Blanton

The best thing to spend on
your child is your time.

Anonymous

The best way for a child to learn to pray is to live with a father and mother who know a life of friendship with God and who truly pray.

J.H. Pestalozzi

A baby is born with the need to be loved
and never outgrows it.

Anonymous

A mother's patience is like a tube of
toothpaste — never quite all gone.

Anonymous

_____

_____

_____

_____

_____

_____

_____

_____

_____

_____

_____

_____

_____

_____

_____

_____

_____

_____

_____

_____

_____

_____

_____

_____

_____

*A baby is a masterpiece painted above
and framed when a family surrounds it with love.*

Anonymous

*T*ell your children about Me. Impress on their hearts how much you love Me. Talk about Me at home when you are doing everyday things like taking a walk or taking a nap.

Deuteronomy 6:6, 7

A baby is
  ...unwritten history
    ...unfathomed mystery.

J.G. Holland

Being a full-time mother is one of the highest salaried jobs in my field, since the payment is pure love.

Mildred B. Vermont

It's not easy being a mother.
If it were easy, fathers would do it.

All your children will be taught by the Lord,
and great will be their peace.

Isaiah 54:13

_____

_____

_____

_____

_____

_____

_____

_____

_____

_____

_____

_____

_____

_____

_____

_____

_____

_____

_____

_____

_____

_____

_____

_____

_____

A Letter to My Child...

*We will never know how much God really loves us,
but having a child certainly gives us a clue.*

Anonymous

A child reaches for your hand
and touches your heart.

Before I formed you in the womb I knew you.

Jeremiah 1:5

An alarm clock is a device
for awakening people who
don't have small children.

Anonymous

*A mother never quite leaves her children at home,
even when she doesn't take them along.*

Margaret Culkin Banning

_____

_____

_____

_____

_____

_____

_____

_____

_____

_____

_____

_____

_____

_____

_____

_____

_____

_____

_____

_____

_____

_____

_____

_____

The sweetest kick you will ever
get is from the inside.

Anonymous

God sends children to enlarge our hearts,
and to make us unselfish and full of
kindly sympathies and affections.

Mary Howitt

Whoever said women were the weaker
sex never witnessed childbirth.

Anonymous

_____
_____
_____
_____
_____
_____
_____
_____
_____
_____
_____
_____
_____
_____
_____
_____
_____
_____
_____
_____
_____
_____
_____
_____
_____
_____
_____

Our children need our presence more than our presents.

Jesse Jackson

One of the most important things about infant care is to never change diapers in midstream.

Don Marquis

*And the child grew in wisdom, stature and
in favor with God and men.*

Luke 2:52

_____
_____
_____
_____
_____
_____
_____
_____
_____
_____
_____
_____
_____
_____
_____
_____
_____
_____
_____
_____
_____
_____
_____
_____
_____
_____
_____
_____

Love and pregnancy and
riding on a camel cannot be hid.

Ancient Proverb

$\mathcal{R}$emember to…
Create moments
Make memories
Shape destinies.

Nancy Gordon

*O*ur children are living messages we send
to a time and place we will not see.

Anonymous

*C*hildren are God's apostles, day by day sent forth to
preach of love and hope and peace.

James Russell Lowell

A Final Letter to My Child...

See you soon!
Love,
Mom